The Beginner's Guide to the 3D Printing Galaxy

By the 3D Printing Professor

Joe Larson

GW00492828

©2017 3D Printing Professor LLC, Joe Larson

All rights reserved. This book or any portion thereof may not be reproduced or used in any manner whatsoever without the express written permission of the publisher except for the use of brief quotations in a book review.

Printed in the United States of America

First Printing, 2017

Ver 0.1

ISBN 9781522014959

3D Printing Professor LLC

www.3dpprofessor.com

Table of Contents

Introduction

Video link: https://www.youtube.com/watch?v=CM-T0i-vbwY

There are many types of people who will benefit from this book.

Those who know very little about 3D printing, but are so excited about the idea that they want to get into it right now will find the background information they need to cut through the hype and get into the reality of 3D printing.

If you don't yet own a 3D printer but really like the idea, this series will also cover how to get the 3D prints you want and need. It will even cover how to get others to do the 3D printing for you. If you do want to buy a 3D printer, this book will cover the essential questions you need to ask before making that purchase.

For those who have already bought a 3D printer, but are having a hard time getting started with it, this book will provide critical information for getting over those difficult first steps. Modern 3D printers, especially the cheaper ones, can be frustrating to use at times and it takes a combination of art and engineering to get the most out of them.

How to Read This Book

You may not want, or need, to read this book cover-to-cover. Nor may you need to read the whole thing. The content in this book casts a fairly wide net, so chances are there are chapters that won't apply to you as much as others. Feel free to pick and choose, whatever you find useful.

Safety is always first and it's good to know the potential dangers associated with 3D printing, so that will be the first chapter. Next, we'll lay down some basic knowledge and define what 3D printing actually is (and isn't).

If you haven't already bought a 3D printer, the next chapter is a *Reality Check* to ensure you really want to do this thing. You don't have to own a 3D printer to use 3D printing, and the chapter "3D Printing Without a 3D Printer" will cover what you need to know about that. It helps to know what kinds of 3D printing technologies are out there, so the chapter titled "Types of 3D Printing" will cover that. If you buy your own 3D printer, it will probably use a technology known as FFF, which stands for Fused Filament Fabrication (or FDM for Fused Deposition Modeling, both of which are the same thing) and so it'll be good to know a little bit about that process.

The last 3 sections will assume you've decided to get a 3D printer for yourself, or that you already have. Congratulations! You'll need to set up both the hardware and software, and we'll cover that. You'll get acquainted with the parts of your FFF 3D printer as well as the parts of the 3D prints it produces, which will help as you try to understand the software side of the 3D printing process.

As you set up the software for a 3D printer you'll discover an app called a "slicer". Even if you don't own a 3D printer you can try out this part of the process right now. We'll go into considerable depth about what slicers do with specific examples of the slicers you'll probably find yourself using.

Finally, we'll discuss where you can find 3D models to print, because what good is a machine that can make anything without something to make?

You might notice as you go that most chapters have a video link after the title. This book started as a series of YouTube video lectures, a bit out of order. These lectures were then transcribed into written in blog posts, and the compiled here. This book, then, represents the best compiled version of this information, with some additional bits not found online. Some people learn best by reading, some people prefer to be talked to, and some prefer hands-on learning. With the video links, book, and example chapters this book should cover them all. Either way, the video links in these chapters can work with the content to enhance your learning experience.

In the end, I hope this book will make 3D printing a reality for you.

1

Safety First

Video link:

https://www.youtube.com/watch?v=FICKkseSMpk

Don't Panic

The purpose of this chapter isn't to scare you away from 3D printing. It is just to make you aware. We deal with potentially dangerous situations every day, big and small. Being aware of the dangers, how we manage those risks, and how we don't, are what make us safer. No one is going to be perfectly safe in every situation, but those who are aware will always be better off.

It's important to realize that 3D printers are machines. And like most machines there are risks associated with their use. Most of these risks are minimal and the number of incidents involving 3D printing are low, especially compared with the number of 3D printers in use. However, unless you're going to only use 3D printing services and let someone else handle the machines, it's still best to start any 3D printing course with a discussion about the safety of 3D printing.

There are many types of 3D printing and each has its own associated risks to take into account. The most common type of 3D printing that you're likely to encounter is Fused Filament Fabrication, or FFF. If the 3D printer you are going to use is a different type than this, like SLA or powder based printers for example, then be sure to familiarize yourself with the safety procedures for using that type of 3D printing.

FFF 3D Printers

1: Finished Prusa Mendel http://reprap.org/wiki/File:Assembled-prusa-mendel.jpg

Good ol' FFF

Most FFF 3D printers that are affordable to most users are not built with safety in mind. They consist of cheaper components and minimal safety features. They tend to be open with moving components and electronics exposed where an unaware person might interact with them. And there tends to be a number of chemicals commonly used with 3D printers that have dangers associated with them. 3D printers, by their nature, also tend to run without supervision, which is when bad things happen.

Fire Danger

3D printers are electrical devices, and electrical wiring, especially when built on the cheap, can spark. A spark can ignite anything flammable. To date, there have been 3 incidents of fires involving 3D printers. In some cases how the 3D printer started the fire is a bit in question. But the point is the users of these printers didn't have safety in mind in their operation.

2: One of the rare fires involving a 3D Printer.
http://s1295.photobucket.com/user/skyminer71/media/House%20Fire/I
MG_1259_zps950e6e59.jpg.html

Many 3D printers have a big power brick on them and for many 3D printers that brick is external. That power brick generates heat and, again potentially, electrical sparks. If the wires leading to the power brick or to the printer get cut, pinched, or damaged, they could heat up, melt, and ignite something around them that could start a fire.

So far, these warnings are true of any electrical devices, but 3D printing has its own unique dangers associated with it.

FFF or FDM 3D printing involves the laying down of layers of melted plastic on top of each other with a mechanical movement system. Plastics are polymers that, when heated, can generate a flammable gas that could be ignited by a spark. Usually 3D printers do not get to the sorts of temperatures required to turn a plastic into a gas, but a broken temperature sensor could cause a heater element to run away with its temperature. Some 3D printers have safeguards to prevent this, but not all do.

If these thermo-polymer plastics do get hot enough to melt and generate heat there is a risk that they will flow, meaning the danger won't be contained to the 3D printer or the area immediately around them. It will quickly spread as the melted plastics flow.

The part of the 3D printer where the material comes out, known as the "hot end", can be the point of ignition if it comes in contact with some foreign material other than the plastic it is meant for, but something else that burns or melts or ignites at a lower temperature than plastic. The hot end can also burn your skin and while hot ends are small and the burn will be minimal, it can still hurt a lot.

Finishing a 3D print often uses common chemicals that are known to be very flammable. Acetone can easily fill an area with flammable gas that is undetectable to the eyes, and since it's heavier than air, will linger far below the nose and may not be detected by smell. Many first-time 3D printer owners use hairspray to adhere prints to their build surface, which uses a propane-based propellant to expel itself from the can. It's important to remember that fire is never safe and should never be played with, no matter how cool it is to watch burn. Always be careful with these materials, and doubly so when around a 3D printer.

Other Dangers

3D printers consist of many moving parts: gears, driving filament and belts, screw leads driving gantries, as well as numerous motors and fans. All of these points are potential pink points for curious fingers or clothes. While the motors that drive most 3D printers aren't strong enough to do any significant damage, and while it's much more likely that the printer will take the brunt of the encounter, there are other printers with stronger motors or points where the torque is more focused. Finger or loose clothes could get caught and pinched.

How to Be Safe

There are some simple, and some more involved things that anyone can do if they're concerned about safety.

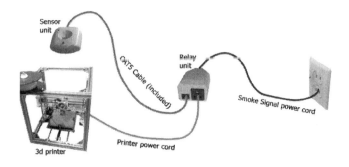

3: "Smoke Signal" a closed loop system for stopping fire in your 3D printer. https://www.kickstarter.com/projects/1064868871/smoke-signal-a-safety-system-for-3d-printers

Among the more involved solutions are systems that attach a sensor to a power relay that will immediately shut down power to your printer in case a potentially hazardous situation is detected. This is an okay solution provided it catches a problem before it becomes more life threatening, but there are very few commercially-available options for this. There are also companies like 3D Print Clean that will build an enclosure for your printer complete with air filtration and fire suppression system designed to deploy in case a fire is detected. These are extreme measures, but ensure a great degree of security concerning your 3D printing.

4: The 3D Print Clean fire suppression system.
http://www.3dprintclean.com/enclosure-fire-suppression-kit.htm

While you are saving up for a system like that, however, consider these simple precautions to safeguarding yourself from the risks of 3D printing:

1. **Keep the area around and near your 3D printer clear of flammable materials**. This includes paper, rags, cloth, insulation, debris, and the chemicals commonly used for 3D printing. Keeping these things near your printer may be convenient, but it's safer to keep them further away.

2. **Use your printer in a well-ventilated area**. This goes double for common finishing chemicals. Always be near a window or door that will open to the outside to clear any vapor or fumes that may be generated in the process of 3D printing.

3. **Have a fire detection system and fire extinguisher near by**.

4. **Use caution around your printer's moving parts**. Keep dangling clothes and fingers, especially little

fingers, away from the 3D printer while it's in motion.

5. **Do not run your 3D printer unattended**. When a machine is left to run unattended, that's when bad things happen. If there's always someone nearby then you can be sure any danger is minimized. Fires can be caught before they start, prints can be turned off before they dramatically fail, and even minor printing errors can be caught quickly.

Maybe at this point you're thinking, "There's no way I can do all these things all the time. The fact that 3D printers can be small, fit on a desk in a small office, and run without you standing over them is the best part about them! How can you expect anyone to never leave their printer unattended or do all these things?"

That's true. No one is perfectly safe in anything. But, again, this section isn't about making you scared or even worried, it's about making you aware. Knowing what you need to do to be safe, and what you are or are not doing, you'll adjust your behavior and be on the lookout for potential pitfalls. Maybe as a result of this you'll change something to be a little safer or you'll think twice about starting a big print before you leave on a long vacation.

As many people that are running cheap, poorly built 3D printers, and as few incidents as there have been with them, home and prosumer FFF 3D printing has a pretty good track record. But you don't want to be the next statistic. 3D printing is fun and I encourage you to have fun with it. Just remember, safety first.

2

What is 3D Printing?

Video Link:
https://www.youtube.com/watch?v=pxh9oXpxNn8

> *The chances of finding out what's really
> going on in the universe are so remote,
> the only thing to do is hang the sense of
> it and keep yourself occupied.*

For people who have only just heard about 3D printing, it can seem like magic. They hear about a machine that sits in your home, and at the push of a button fills up with whatever you want. And every day it seems like someone else is doing something amazing with it. No wonder it has this mystique surrounding it. It's been said that any technology, sufficiently advanced, is indistinguishable from magic.

However, 3D printing obviously isn't magic. It's real, and real things have challenges and limitations associated with them.

What is 3D Printing?

This can be a difficult to answer because 3D printing describes a lot of different processes that all work in similar ways, but each have their own strengths and weaknesses. Generally, 3D printers are computer controlled machines that start with nothing and add to it, building things in a process called "additive manufacturing".

How do 3D Printers do It?

It's true that there's no limit to what 3D printing can do, but that doesn't mean they can do anything. It's important to understand what 3D printing is in order to know what it can and cannot do.

Generally, 3D printers work in layers with each layer stacking on the layer below it. These layers are sometimes so thin it's impossible to see them.

Like building with blocks or bricks, or making piles of snow or sand, if any part doesn't have something beneath it, then plans have to be made to as to how that part will be supported, like building a scaffolding or temporary structure of some sort. Different 3D printers do this in different ways.

Advantages of 3D Printing

Because 3D printers are computer controlled, they can create elegant and repeatable designs with less human interaction. Being additive means that 3D printing generates less waste than other manufacturing processes. Also, being computer controlled it lends itself well to iterative design.

Traditionally, an engineer would make a design plan, send that plan to a shop, and wait for a skilled workman to follow the plans and make the thing real, and then wait again for the object to get shipped back to the engineer. In this process, any change is expensive. "Good enough" often ends up being the best you can hope for. Now, with a 3D printer it's so relatively cheap, fast, and easy to make a change there's no reason not to try the design over and over again until it is exactly the way you want it.

And if a designer makes their tested design available to you, and you have a similar 3D printer, it's a simple matter to print your own. Just calibrate your printer, load it up with filament, prepare the 3D model, and go. All their work and effort in making the design can save you having to do the same. It might not work every time, but when it does it's wonderful.

But is It Magic?

3D printing describes a number of processes, including some machines which could be in your house. With the push of a few buttons, and a little machine operation, they can automatically, additively, make something from a design that possibly someone else created.

Does that sound like magic? Now that it's broken down it's clear that while 3D printing isn't actual magic, it can be pretty magical.

3

Reality Check

Video link:
https://www.youtube.com/watch?v=v8huw5MRU2E

> *"It seemed to me," said Wonko the Sane,*
> *"that any civilization that had so far lost*
> *its head as to need to include a set of*
> *detailed instructions for use in a packet*
> *of toothpicks, was no longer a civilization*
> *in which I could live and stay sane."*

If you already have a 3D printer, you might not need to read this chapter. If you don't have a 3D printer, but think you want one, you may want to think twice.

Of course, the goal of this conversation isn't to convince you that you shouldn't get into 3D printing. Everyone should get into 3D printing. But everyone should also be successful in 3D printing. The goal is to put you on solid footing before starting.

3D printers aren't perfect. They're hardly what could be called turnkey technology right now. 3D printers are very cool, but the hype can sometimes overshadow reality. It's best to have an honest idea of what you're getting into before you start. I hope this only strengthens your resolve to get into 3D printing.

Simply put, you need to know this: 3D printing won't do all the hard work for you. It may save you some labor and produce a better result than you thought possible by any other means, but it will still require work and effort, and probably more of both than you expect. Operating a 3D printer is a hobby. Do you have time for that?

If you're getting a 3D printer because you have a specific project in mind, a 3D printer probably isn't the only thing you need for that project and it's probably not the first thing you need either. You'll need 3D models for the printer, if nothing else. Can you make 3D models? If not, maybe you should start there. Maybe you don't need a 3D printer at all. Maybe you can have someone else print it for you.

My Story

5: Photo Curtesy of Deal Extreme: http://www.dx.com/p/geeetech-reprap-prusa-mendel-i2-3d-printer-blue-349130#.WTh7AGjyuUn

When I first heard about 3D printing it was through the RepRap project and I was immediately hyped. I never knew that there could be a machine that could automatically make things, and suddenly I was being told that they were not only possible but available for only $800 in parts. However, as reasonable as that expense was for the promise, I couldn't afford it while I had a family and kids to support. So, I started saving and, in the meanwhile, I did more research. I say research, but it was more like uncontrollably drooling over any piece of information I could find. I was an insufferable fan.

I'm glad that I held off because I quickly learned that $800 worth of parts was a little misleading. There was another $300 of recommended parts if you wanted a machine that didn't suck, and at least 3 hours to assemble, and a whole weekend to troubleshoot. Most of those early RepRap printers were self-sourced, and if you did manage to get it to work once, there was nothing saying they'd work again.

There was a particular sort of madness to those early 3D printer makers. Of course, you might be able to buy a kit with all the part you needed, ready for you to assemble, but those were often more expensive without being any more reliable or easy, only saving you the headache of self-sourcing. As much as I wanted a 3D printer, I'm glad I waited.

But I was still interested. I had gone to school for computer animation, and so I knew I could make 3D models. I found Blender was the free 3D modeling program du jour. My experiences with Maya and 3DS max made Blender not too difficult to use for me, and I starting modeling and sharing the models I made with the online community of 3D printer owners.

One of the first models I shared online was a Chinese chess set, but made with icons instead of Chinese characters, for those people who are scared by any communicative glyph not in the roman alphabet.

Someone in Massachusetts with a 3D printer contacted me and said that they were going to print my model. I asked if he'd print me a set as well. He quoted me a price for it which seemed a little high for a Chinese chess set, but he had the 3D printer and I realized this couldn't be compared to the price of a mass-manufactured set at all. It was custom manufacturing.

6: https://pinshape.com/items/604-3d-printed-iconified-xiangqi-set-chinese-chess

The first time I held in my hand a design I had made in the computer, brought to life with a machine, my fate was sealed. Of course, there were things about this model that weren't quite right. For instance, the raised line near the horse's neck was 1mm thick, which I thought was fine. But I discovered that a 1mm wall is 3D printed with a gap if you're using a 4mm nozzle, by necessity. It was the sort of thing that I wouldn't have learned without actually printing it.

I kept designing and entered several contests, eventually winning the grand prize in one contest and netting myself a 3D printer of my very own.

I'm grateful I took a slow approach to getting into 3D printing, and so I recommend that approach to everyone. The longer you take to get into it, the longer you'll probably stick with it.

My story isn't yours. Many people have jumped into 3D printing without counting the cost and are still going strong today. Nowadays 3D printers are more affordable and user-friendly than ever. There are more 3D modeling software options than there were when I started, and they are so much easier to use that maybe waiting doesn't make sense.

Do a little research, and hopefully you'll still decide to take the plunge.

4

3D Printing Without a 3D Printer

Video link:
https://www.youtube.com/watch?v=SRF3n6sSJdY

*A common mistake that people make
when trying to design something
completely foolproof is to underestimate
the ingenuity of complete fools.*

Again, if you already own a 3D printer you probably don't
need this chapter. But if you don't have a 3D printer you can
still take advantage of 3D printing to make cool things and
solve problems. And you don't have to break the bank to do
it. You just have to have a little bit of knowledge about 3D

printing processes to get the most from it. The key is the more you can do yourself, the more you'll be able to save.

The first question is: where will your 3D models come from? How exactly to find 3D models will be covered in a later chapter, but it's important to know where you're getting the models to 3D print.

Downloading a model online generally is the cheapest and easiest way to get started. Sometimes you can even be sure the model works because you can see that others have printed it. There are tens of thousands of 3D models available online. For some people, wanting to print a specific model that they saw online is what got them started in 3D printing.

But maybe what you want to print hasn't been modeled yet. In that case it might be best to do the modeling yourself. Hiring a designer can be very costly. So learning a 3D modeling program and using it will save a lot of money. How to model for 3D printing will be covered in later books.

If you're doing a project for an organization that can afford it, then hire a designer. They'll produce professional quality models that you can have confidence will work.

Now that the topic of where models will come from has been covered, let's get back to how to get them 3D printed.

Know the Different Types of 3D Printing

There are different types of 3D printing, knowing which one will work best for your model may limit how you can 3D print it. Each type of 3D printing has its strengths and weaknesses. What you're trying to print may not work well with the printing process you're hoping to use, and using the wrong type of 3D printer can result in an unsatisfactory result.

Some models work well with the cheapest 3D printing process, FFF 3D printing. Others that require internal support, or have thin parts or complex shapes may require a process that has less restrictions but will come at a higher cost or take longer to produce.

If you don't already have a lot of knowledge about this topic, an in-depth exploration of the different types of 3D printing will occupy a whole chapter later.

Know Your 3D Model and What Printing Process It Will Work With

If a model was not designed with the limitations of a specific 3D printing process in mind, it may be a challenge to get an acceptable print out of it.

For instance, printing in FFF works best with a flat bottom, gentle overhangs, and, when supports are necessary, the more contact area with the supports, the better. But for other 3D printing processes, making walls too thin, or not taking into account tolerances that are necessary for parts to meet well can result in needing to redesign and reprint.

Expecting a part that can stand up to the rigors of everyday use from a process that produces fragile parts, such as some powder binding processes, can also result in disappointment. So, it is important to be at least a little aware of the limitations of the 3D printing process you're going to use.

Of course, if the model already exists before and someone has successfully printed it, you can have the greatest confidence in its success. However, any untested model will have a degree of risk associated with it. With any untested model it's probably a good idea to expect at least one redesign. Still, a little knowledge will go a long way towards saving on reprints and money.

Volume Generally Affects Price the Most

The size that a 3D model will be when printed is usually the biggest factor in determining price. Most printing services calculate price by starting with a setup fee, then adding cost based on volume. As things get a little bigger, the price goes up considerably. For example, if a 3D model is made twice as big, it's not just wider. It's also longer and taller. Consider a cube, then consider how many cubes would fit inside a cube that was double in size.

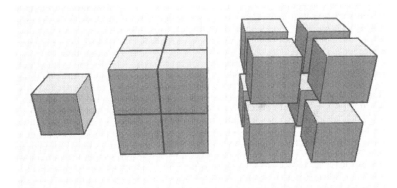

The new cube is eight times the volume of the original! So, a 3D model that has double the size may cost eight times as much to print.

Most CAD or 3D modeling software have tools to calculate the volume of the part. Many slicers (which we will cover later) also have tools for calculating volume. In lieu of complex tools, simply measuring the height, width, and length of the model and multiplying them together can give an idea of the volume.

Tricks like hollowing out your model, making it smaller, or combining multiple parts into a single print may be appropriate for different service providers, depending on the 3D printer they use. So some experimentation may be necessary to get the best price.

Estimate Your Price

Now that you know what process you're going to shop for and the volume of the print, the next step is to estimate the price. 3D printing services tend to be closed-lipped about their specific printing prices and the factors that they consider, which may include material being used, whether supports are necessary, and if any post processing will be needed.

Generally, 3D printing on a home or prosumer FFF in ABS or PLA is the cheapest, many people only charging a little more than the cost of materials. Professional FDM printing is the next most expensive but they can print almost anything with dissolvable supports. The next most expensive are services that use uses a powder process 3D printer like selective laser sintering (SLS) or liquid polymerization processes like stereolithography (SLA). SLS has fewer design restrictions as well and SLA processes capture fine details the best. Direct Metal Laser Sintering (DMLS) are often the most expensive because they produce parts that are rugged and could be used in professional applications.

Shop Around

There are many 3D printing services available. Many are set up to give you an instant estimate online. Going through these services is quick and easy, but you'll sometimes pay a premium for that ease. By far the cheapest way to get 3D prints is usually a tried and true method known as "I know a guy".

Home and prosumer FFF 3D printers are more available than ever. Chances are someone in your area has one. But you have to find them. Some are listed on sites like 3D Hubs or MakeXYZ. For others a web search for "3D Printer" and your area will turn up some surprising results. More and more colleges and local libraries have 3D printers that the public can use. An online search will find them. Look for maker meetups in your area and see who attends. Building a personal relationship with someone who has a 3D printer is the best way to get 3D prints without the expense of a 3D printer. I don't know anyone who has a 3D printer that will say no if you hand them an STL to print, especially if you have some confidence that it will print on their printer. Plus, having someone local can often save on shipping.

Of course, all this planning isn't worth a thing without the last step.

Pull the Trigger

Go ahead and make the purchase. Even if it's a little more than you expected, get over that sticker shock and make the purchase. Don't compare the price to a comparable mass manufactured item. 3D printing is custom manufacturing made on demand. Expect that it will cost a little more. Plus, it's still cheaper than buying a 3D printer. So do it, make the purchase.

There is nothing more educational about 3D printing than actually holding a physical print in your hand. Seeing how the model is translated by the 3D printing process, discovering its nuances and limitations by exploring a print will provide you information that no book or video will. 3D printing isn't a theoretical process, it's real and has to be made real to understand it. And making it real will be the best way to decide if you need to buy a 3D printer.

But owning a 3D printer is not the only way to use 3D printing. Holding off on the expense of a 3D printer, both in time and learning, will give you more information about whether 3D printing is for you. Maybe, once 3D printing is made real for you you'll decide that it isn't worth it and you'll be glad you didn't start by buying a 3D printer.

On the other hand, maybe you'll look into this first print and see 100 more prints down the road, in which case owning your own 3D printer will be the best decision you ever made.

Additional reading:

http://www.3ders.org/articles/20160721-how-do-suppliers-calculate-pricing-for-3d-prints.html

5

Types of 3D Printing

Video link:
https://www.youtube.com/watch?v=SRF3n6sSJdY

*Eskimos had over two hundred different
words for snow, without which their
conversation would probably have got
very monotonous.*

3D printing describes a large number of technologies, all of
which do similar things, but in different ways.

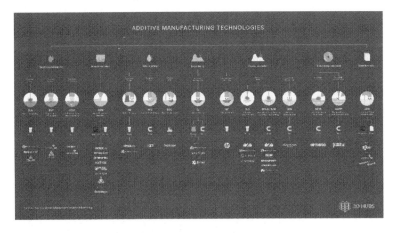

3D Hubs made an excellent illustration of the many
different 3D printing technologies out there, and with their
permission this chapter will use it for illustrative purposes.

Vat Polymerization

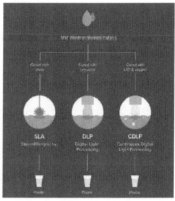

The first type of 3D printing ever developed involved a vat of a liquid that turned solid when exposed to UV light. The process as developed exposed this liquid to light in selective ways, then pulled that layer out, then exposing the liquid to light again for the shape of the next layer. This can be done with a fine laser drawing on the surface of the liquid or a whole layer at a time could be exposed with a projector. There are still a number of 3D printers that use this method.

These light-cured prints can be very high in detail. However, it has a few disadvantages. For one, you can only use a single material type. Also, liquid polymers can be hard to work with and are often mildly toxic. These printers tend to be expensive and the light-curing resin is also expensive, which makes these printers expensive to own and operate.

Fused Deposition Modeling or Fused Filament Fabrication

The next 3D printing technology ever invented is Fused Deposition Modeling (FDM) or Fused Filament Fabrication (FFF). Both describe a process where a material is melted, extruded from a nozzle, and deposited layer-by-layer on a build surface, but FDM and Fused Deposition Modeling are trademarks of Stratasys, so the hobby community devised an alternate term.

FFF 3D printing has quickly become the most common type of 3D printing. If you have a 3D printer in your home or business, it's probably going to be one of these types of 3D printers. It is also one of the most mature 3D printing technologies with a wide variety of materials. Some FFF 3D printers can even use more than one material in the same print, including the possibility of building a support in a different material that is easier to remove cleanly.

FFF 3D printing is also one of the most rapidly advancing 3D printing technologies with new innovations coming out constantly.

There are high-end industrial FFF 3D printers that cost hundreds of thousands of dollars, and lower end home machines that cost a few hundred. The materials for these printers tend to be cheap as well, making FFF 3D printing perhaps the most affordable option overall.

Because FFF 3D printing tends to take place with nothing but air around it, it can be very susceptible to environmental changes, like a sudden breeze when a door is opened too quickly. Also, it tends to be limited in the amount of detail it can produce, though it often produces more than enough detail for most applications.

Home FFF 3D printers tend to suffer from a lack of quality control and calibrating them properly is left to the user, making them some of the most hands-on printers to use.

Material Jetting

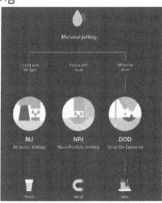

Material jetting is where a liquid is selectively deposited, similar to an inkjet printer, into a reservoir of some agent that absorbs it, then a new layer of the agent is added and printed on layer by layer, on top of the previous.

Some processes work in open air instead of a reservoir of material, laying down liquid polymers then curing them to a solid with light, then building the layers on top of that, similar to FFF 3D printing. It might even be the same light-curing materials used in vat polymerization, but with no vat. Or it might be a process that cures with heat.

3D printers that use this technology are controlled by a handful of companies, but they are doing some very cool things with them such as combining multiple materials with different properties in the same print, and even mixing them to make parts of the print with a blend of the different properties of both materials.

As these technologies are controlled by only a few companies, they are very expensive to own and operate at this time.

Binder Jetting

Very similar to material jetting, binder jetting selectively lays down a liquid binder into a reservoir of a base material. The liquid binder holds the base material together like glue. Then a thin layer of material is added and binder is again applied to build the print layer by layer.

Binder jetting can produce full-color prints with colored binders. And because binder jetting works with a reservoir that fills up completely there's no need to worry about supports and complex prints are possible with ease. Simply pull the bound print out of the dust-like base material when the print is done.

The disadvantages of binder jetting is that it requires a place to build the print, and a place to keep the material for building the print, that are both likely the same size, making binder jetting 3D printers bulky. Plus the dust-like build material is messy, meaning this isn't the sort of technology to be brought into your home.

Binder jetting is also one of the more expensive printing options as it, too, is controlled by just a few companies.

Still, binder jetting is a very cool technology that can do things that other 3D printing technologies cannot.

Powder Bed Fusion

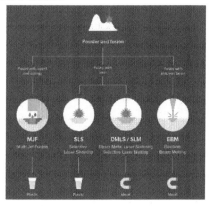

Powder bed fusion has a lot in common with binder jetting. Again, a reservoir is filled up with a dust-like base material. But this time instead of selectively adding a liquid to glue the material together, the material is melted together. Some versions of powder bed fusion use a liquid that then causes a curing process to target where the liquid was added, but the process is the same: it's melting the material together.

Other powder bed fusion processes use high-powered lasers to melt plastic or even metal. This creates a part that is so strong and functional that functional airplane parts have been made with this process.

Powder bed fusion is very industrial and very functional. It is also very expensive. High-powered lasers and metal powder are not cheap. And like binder jetting it's messy with a lot of fine powder surrounding the finished product.

Direct Energy Deposition

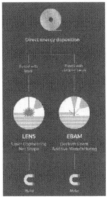

A relatively new comer to the 3D printing arena, direct energy deposition, is a little like CNC welding in 3D. Instead of a filament of plastic like FFF, a filament of metal welds layer-by-layer.

Direct energy deposition prints tend to be a somewhat imprecise and look a little rough because of the nature of the process, but there are companies trying to counteract this by adding a grinding process after the layer goes down to clean up the edges. This is still a very new technology and relatively untested in terms of effectiveness and economics.

Sheet Lamination

Finally, there is sheet lamination. A cool combination of 2D and 3D printing. A sheet of paper is laid down, optionally colored with a traditional printing process, then cut to the shape of the layer and a glue is added. Then another piece of paper is added, cut, glued, and so forth until the print is complete. Simply break the print out of the block of paper in the end.

Sheet lamination creates high detail, full-color prints. However, as the parts are made of paper, even though it's more like a block of wood after the print, the results aren't as durable as other materials.

Sheet lamination is also a newer technology and the price of ownership and operation is still a little high, but who knows what the future holds for this technology?

Which 3D Printing Technology is Right?

What 3D printing technology will you choose to use for your project? It depends on what your project is and what you have available to you.

This book will deal mostly with FFF 3D printing because it is the most economic and commonly available. While home SLA printers also exist, as well as new technology coming out all the time, it is still most likely the 3D printer that you have in your home will be FFF based, so it's probably best to do a deeper dive into how FFF 3D printing does what it does.

6

The FFF Printing Process

Video link: https://www.youtube.com/watch?v=w-e-SQk-wmM

All you really need to know for the moment is that the universe is a lot more complicated than you might think, even if you start from a position of thinking it's pretty ... complicated in the first place.

Your first 3D printer is likely to be a FFF or FDM type of printer. Both work on the same principle:, melting a material and depositing it in 3D space, layer by layer. In this chapter, we'll be going in-depth about how FFF 3D printers do their thing.

The FFF 3D printing process actually starts with a piece of software called a **slicer**. A slicer is a software program that takes a 3D model and turns it into the instructions that the 3D printer follows to make an object. The slicer software could be running on a computer embedded into the 3D printer. However, to save money, most 3D printers use your computer to run the slicing software.

Slicers generally can't create the 3D models. You either have to download the 3D model from a website or design it in another piece of software, sometimes called CAD software.

A slicer creates its instructions by taking a 3D model and figuring out what each layer will look like, then deciding what motion the 3D printer will need to follow to create that "slice" of a layer. The output of a slicer is a set of instructions called **GCode.** When the 3D printer follows those instructions it should make a real version of the 3D model given to the slicer. GCode includes instructions to control every aspect of what the 3D printer does including moving the nozzle, feeding plastic, turning the heaters on or off, turning the fans on or, waiting for the heaters to reach a certain temperature, etc. It's a complicated dance, and it's all created by the slicer.

Once the slicer has created the GCode, those instructions need to be transferred to the 3D printer. That can be accomplished across a USB connection, via an SD card or USB stick, or in some of the fancier printers, even across Wi-Fi.

Once the instructions are in the 3D printer, it activates to follow them and the **movement system** springs to life. FFF 3D printers have a system of motors designed to move in three directions; left-and-right (along the **X-Axis**), forward-and-backward (along the **Y-Axis**) and up-and-down (along the **Z-Axis**). Different 3D printers accomplish this movement in different ways. Some move the build platform along the

Y-axis while moving the nozzle along the X- and Z-axes. Others move the X and Y together at the top of the printer while the build plate moves up and down. Delta printers keep the build plate stationary while the nozzle does all the movement in the X, Y, and Z. However it is accomplished, the whole point is to move the hot end around in relation to the build plate.

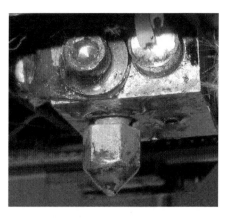

The **hot end** is where the plastic filament comes out. It's little more than a nozzle with a little hole in it to squirt out plastic, attached to a heater element to get the plastic nice and hot, along with a temperature sensor to make sure doesn't get the plastic too hot. The whole point of the system is to melt and focus the plastic that is fed into it.

FFF 3D printers use plastic, generally, that has been prepared by making it into a thin noodle called **filament**. Filament is generally wound around a spool so it can be fed easily into the 3D printer. Filament usually comes in one of two standard sizes: 1.75 mm and 3mm (which actually measures 2.85mm). Most FFF 3D printers are set up, with rare exception, to use one or the other, but not both. It's important to know what size your 3D printer uses so you don't accidentally buy filament you can't use.

Filament is drawn into the 3D printer and down into the hot end by the **feed system**. The feed system is another motor driven component that uses a toothed gear to grab and pull the filament, with a system to push the filament against that feeder gear so it doesn't slip. Some have additional gears to trade torque for speed if necessary.

Some feed systems are close to the nozzle and are carried around with the hot end. Others are very far away from the hot end.

It's good to know where the feed system is in relation to the hot end. If the feed system is far from the hot end, the movement system only needs to move the hot end around, reducing the weight it needs to carry. But this system relies on the stiffness of the filament to carry the motion through to the hot end. If you're using a softer material, like flexible filaments, and there's a gap in the system, the flexible filament can go squishing out the wrong direction, potentially even winding itself around the feed system. The way your feed system is set up can limit what your 3D printer can do.

So far, we've covered how the slicer creates the instructions the 3D printer follows, the movement system that moves the hot end around, and the filament that is driven by the feed system. Finally, it's time to talk about where it all goes.

The **build plate** is a flat surface where the plastic is deposited layer by layer. The build plate may be the most important part of an FFF 3D printer when it comes to the success of a print because it needs to hold to the print while printing is happening, and release it after the print is done. If it releases too soon, the print will fail; if it doesn't release after the print is done it can be very frustrating and ruin a print.

Some build plates are heated, some are not. Some people use hairspray and glass, others use more exotic materials like polyetherimide (PEI) or materials manufactured for the purpose of being a 3D printing build plate, like BuildTak. Still others use disposable build plates designed to be consumed in the process.

Where Did It Go Wrong?

If a print fails, it could be the fault of any of these parts. So it helps to be well-acquainted with the whole system to diagnose print problems.

Now, let's look at how a 3D print is built by the printer.

7

Anatomy of An FFF Print

Video link:
https://www.youtube.com/watch?v=1HpHw4fbhUk

> *Isn't it enough to see that a garden is
> beautiful without having to believe that
> there are fairies at the bottom of it too?*

So now that we've talked about the 3D printer, let's take apart a 3D print for a closer look.

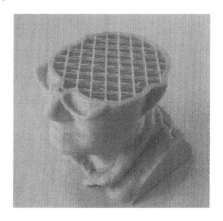

Here is a 3D print that was stopped before it completed. Looking inside this print the parts of an FFF 3D print can be seen.

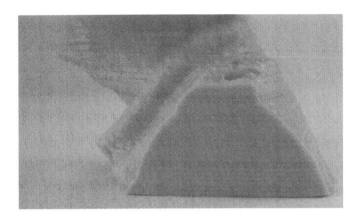

FFF 3D prints are made in **layers**. The lowest layer is the first, the next layer goes on top of that, and so on to the top.

Each layer starts with an **outline**, or **shell**, which traces the shape of the layer one or more times. The more shells, the thicker the wall of the print. With fewer shells, time and material is saved but makes a less rigid and lighter weight print.

Once the shells are drawn there is an **infill** pattern drawn next. Notice that this 3D print is mostly hollow, which is typical. This also saves material and time. Of course, the bottom few layers are completely filled in and a number of top layers are as well, but the layers in between are a sparse infill. Some prints will work successfully without any infill, but if there are any flat areas then infill provides the bridging required to create a smooth top, though it may take a number of top layers to be successful.

FFF 3D prints are made in layers, with each layer building on the one below it. If there is a portion of a model that would print without anything underneath it, the print may require supports.

The wizard model shown here, when it prints, gets to a number of areas wherein the layer gets up to them, but has nothing under them. FFF 3D printers can't print a structure suspended in midair, so a scaffolding structure was built up to that part.

If the supports are made of the same material as the object, because the printer is the type that can only print using one material, these supports are called "breakaway supports", as they are designed to break away after printing completes. The goal of breakaway supports is to make them thin and fragile, but not too thin and fragile because they need to stay until they're no longer needed. Usually breakaway supports leave some artifact behind, a scar that will need to be cleaned off before the print can be truly presentable.

Some 3D printers make their supports out of a different material than the build material. Usually this different material is designed to be dissolved away after the print finishes and it can be made much more solid. Dissolvable supports often leave no artifacts that they were ever there, making supported surfaces as clean as top surfaces. But printers that can use dissolvable supports, and use them well, are more expensive than single material printers.

Some 3D prints don't require any supports. A clever 3D designer can make a part friendly to the FFF process by ensuring that each layer has something under it to support. That may mean orienting the piece in clever ways, breaking the print into parts that each print well, then can be assembled together after, or other clever design considerations.

Layers, outlines, infill, and supports. That's really all there is to FFF 3D prints. However, even these simple parts allow for a great volume and combination of settings that need to be considered in the slicer, which will be the topic of later chapters.

8

A 3D Printer at Home (or Work)

It said that the planet of NowWhat had been named after the opening words of the first settlers to arrive there after struggling across light years of space to reach the farthest unexplored outreaches of the Galaxy.

So, you've decided a 3D printer is for you. You've done your research, made your purchase, and you've got a big box in front of you.

Now what?

Finding a Home

The first question you need to decide is where the printer will be. 3D printers, as mentioned in the *Safety First* chapter, need to be in a room with proper ventilation and away from flammables. A closet or place where other things are stored probably isn't the best choice. 3D printers also often create a little noise when they are running, so putting them in the main area where people congregate frequently is also probably not the best choice.

Some 3D printers need a dedicated computer to run them, though many can run without a computer, so be sure to research what else your printer requires. Environmental elements can also be a concern. If a garage or shed isn't insulated or even partially climate controlled it can cause prints to fail.

Clearly choosing the ideal location isn't easy, and chances are any location you choose will have compromises to be made. You're not looking for a perfect location, just the best location you can. Also keep in mind that while most 3D printers aren't "portable", they can be moved. Whatever you choose doesn't need to be your printer's final resting place. Just get a place for now, but be willing to think twice about it later.

Setting Up the Hardware

Naturally the next step is to unpack the printer and introduce it to its new home. Depending on what you decided on, you might have a complete printer or a kit that you have to build.

Either way the first thing to look for when opening the box is the instructions. This seems obvious, but sometimes 3D printer manufacturers save on paper by including only digital copies of their manual. If you don't see a printed manual, look for an SD card or USB stick. It may be the same SD card that is already loaded in the printer. Put that card or stick in your computer first and check to see if the manufacturer loaded the latest version of the manual and the software you will need to set up there. Once you've found the manual, follow it to set up your printer.

Setting up the Software

Most 3D printers have a software component that needs to be installed. This is the slicer mentioned in previous chapters. It takes the 3D models and turns them into the instructions that the 3D printer will follow.

Some 3D printer manufacturers have written their own slicer software. Others use a generic slicer that can be downloaded online and is designed for general purpose use. Either way there will usually be a recommendation from your manufacturer. If you're a beginner that is probably your best choice for now. Install the recommended slicer, and you're ready to go.

It's best to think of the slicer as a part of your 3D printer. It's just a part that resides on your computer instead of the actual 3D printer. Slicers are in fact a critical part of your 3D printer and it wouldn't be able to print anything without them. However, they can also be confusing, which is why the next several chapters are devoted to explaining their settings and helping you use the most common of them.

9

Slicer Settings

Video link:
https://www.youtube.com/watch?v=RnnXsC4T7Ug

Here I am, brain the size of a planet, and they ask me to pick up a piece of paper.

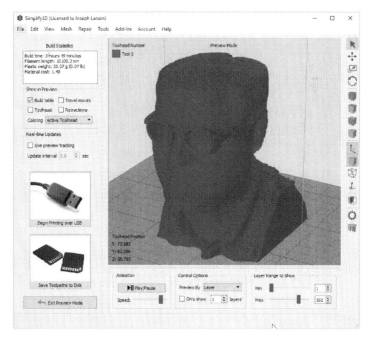

The great thing about slicers is even if you don't have the hardware of a 3D printer, you can have the software part of a 3D printer on your computer right now to practice a little bit of 3D printing.

As stated before, slicers are a special piece of software that turns a 3D model into instructions that a 3D printer can follow to make a 3D print. Slicers take 3D models, often in the form of STL files, but sometimes other formats like OBJ or 3MF. Most slicers allow some simple manipulation of the 3D object, like scaling, rotating, and positioning where they will print.

The output slicers generally produce is called **GCode**, which is a special control language the 3D printer follows to create the print. Most 3D printers do this almost blindly. It's like the slicer is creating a treasure map for someone who is going to be blind and deaf while following it.

Once the print is started there's very little about a print that will change from the instructions in the GCode. So slicers have a great deal to do with the success or failure of your 3D prints.

While there are many different slicers to choose from, there are currently three that are most common and work for many different 3D printers:

- Cura (https://ultimaker.com/en/products/cura-software)
- Simplify3D (https://www.simplify3d.com/)
- Slic3r (http://slic3r.org/)

Each slicer is created by a different group of people, and so, are slightly different in how they turn 3D models into prints. But they also have many significant things in common, since all FFF 3D prints still have all the same parts: layers shells, infill, and supports.

First Time Setup

If you decide to load a slicer before you own a 3D printer, you will discover that you do need to choose *a* 3D printer when you set up the slicer software. The GCode produced for one 3D printer will not work in a different 3D printer. But if you don't have a 3D printer it really doesn't matter what make and model you set the software up for. Just choose one or go with the defaults for now. Most slicers that can handle many different printers allow for adding additional printers later, so you can always change.

If you do own a specific 3D printer, the steps for setting up the slicer for your printer should be included in the instructions that came with your printer.

Slicer Settings

The chapter after this one will have some hands-on practice to follow along with. For now, here's an overview of the settings all slicers have in common that you're likely to have to consider. If you ever have a question about the settings you see, you can always refer to this chapter.

Layer Height

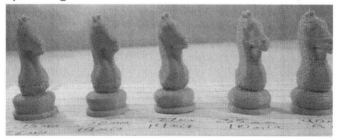

Layer height defines how thick or thin each layer is. A higher number means thicker layers which will print faster but will produce rougher sides to your print, like a washboard. On the other hand, a thinner layer will print much slower but result in a much better-looking print.

Experimenting with layer thickness can have consequences. Some people like to push their layer thickness as low as possible, but if the nozzle doesn't move up enough between each layer there's a chance that the plastic, when it comes out, may not have enough space to flow and will result in a jam. Experiment with caution.

A layer height of 0.15mm-0.2mm is generally recommended.

Shell/Outline/Wall Thickness

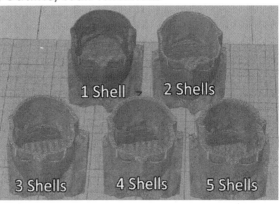

Each layer of a print starts by outlining the shape. This is sometimes called a shell or the outer wall.

Each shell is drawn slightly inside the others, so the number of shells determines how thick the outside walls of your print will be. More shells create a heavier, more rigid print and use more material.

Common values for this setting is 2 or 3 shells, or about 0.8mm-1.2mm thick.

Top and Bottom Layers

The bottom of your print is always printed completely filled in. But how many layers should be laid down like that before getting to the sparse infill? There's a setting for that. Before topping off a print, how many layers should be built up so that the print has time to cover the infill properly? That's also a setting.

For most slicers this is a number, but some slicers like to take this as a measurement and calculate it for you.

Top layers can be very important to the appearance of a print. If the infill pattern can be seen on the top of a print then chances are more top layers are necessary. Often times while only 3-6 layers are advisable for the bottom, more than twice that is recommended for the top, or 6-12 layers.

Infill

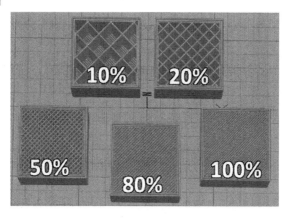

Slicers allow control over the shape and amount of infill. **Infill percentage** defines how dense the fill inside a print is. 100% infill is a solid print, and 0% would be completely hollow.

If a solid part is desired, 80% infill is close enough to solid for most applications, and can overcome problems with over extrusion that can be compounded by attempting to print something at 100% fill.

The lower the infill setting is, the less plastic will be wasted on the part of a print that no one will see. However, since the infill is what the top layers print on, if the top layers are not looking good increasing infill can be another way to fix them. Some models will even print well with 0% infill, if they don't have large, flat tops but come to a point.

In general, a value between 10%-20% is common.

Support Settings

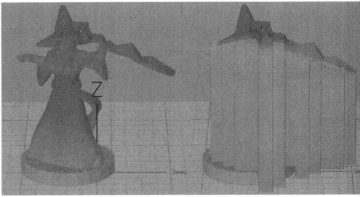

Next are the settings to control where and how to apply overhang support, the scaffolding structure to give the parts of a print that would hang free midair something to print on. The biggest variation between different slicers is in the support settings. Fine-tuning supports for individual models is sometimes an art as much as a science. The most common type of supports are called "break-away" supports because after printing these supports must be broken away from the object.

You can tell the slicer what **angle** to look for surfaces that need support. That is to say if a part is going out gradually at a gentle overhang, it will usually not need supports, but if it is going out more parallel to the build platform, or even overhanging, it may require supports to succeed. So you can tell the slicer what angle to look for to start building supports up to a part.

Under the support structure settings there is often a setting that asks if you want supports everywhere or only "**from the build plate**". This is if the part needing support is directly over the build plate, or if there's another part of the print under it. Switching this setting to only make supports from the build plate can eliminate internal support structures that may be hard to remove, but it may fail to support a part that needs it. Use this setting with judgement, as every print will need to be carefully looked over by a human eye to see if it will succeed.

There are also settings for the **density** of the support and the **gap**. Like infill, a higher setting will create more support structures and will support overhanging parts better, but if it's too dense it will also be difficult to remove after. The gap describes how much space the slicer leaves between the support and the part to help with removal of the support. A gap of 0 may fuse the support to the part making them impossible to remove.

Generally, supporting parts that are more than 45 degrees, or a 50% grade, is advisable. Although when building supports, sometimes a value as high as 60% will make sure everything is covered. 70% density on the supports will ensure that everything is covered well and there's not much gap between for failure points, and a 0.3mm horizontal gap will make sure that it doesn't stick to side surfaces it's not supposed to.

Filament Diameter

While diameter of your filament is generally determined by what your printer uses, different filaments from different suppliers can be slightly thicker or thinner within the tolerances of your printer. While this won't affect your printer, it will affect your prints. Slightly thicker filament means that it's pushing more plastic out every time it feeds, making the noodle of plastic that the printer is drawing with thicker, throwing off the measured accuracy of your prints by ever so little. Likewise, slightly thinner filament may result in not enough plastic being put out resulting in poor layer adhesion, and loose tolerances on the finished part.

It's recommended to measure your filament and adjust this setting to get accurate prints. If prints don't need to be accurate, going with the standard filament diameters, 1.75mm or 2.85mm, depending on your printer, is usually fine.

Flow Rate

While accurately measured filament will tell the slicer how much or little plastic to put out, there may be other factors to consider, like the density of the material. Sometimes an accurate measurement doesn't fix the problem. So slicers have a "fudge" factor that can be used to alter the **flow rate**. It's measured as a percentage, though it's sometimes a percentage expressed in decimal, in other words, 1 for

100%, 0.5 for 50%, etc. Usually this setting can be left at 100%, but some materials, like PLA, sometimes do better at 90%.

Nozzle Diameter

The nozzle at the end of the hot end has a hole in it and the size of that hole determines how thin a noodle of plastic you'll be printing with, which in turn determines how small a detail you can print. The nozzle is a part that can be changed, so your 3D printer needs to know how big that hole is. A bigger nozzle hole diameter will allow for faster prints and thicker layers with less fine detail.

Nozzles commonly have a hole diameter of 0.4mm, but check with your printer manufacturer before changing this setting. Also, if you change your nozzle you are responsible for alerting the slicer to the change.

Temperature

What temperature you print at is mostly determined by what material you're using. Printing hotter will result in more easy flow through the nozzle, but getting it too hot may cause the filament to melt too far up the feed tube and cause a jam. This is often called "heat creep". It's best to figure out what the very edge of the filament's melting point is and keep the temperature there.

Some 3D printers have heated build plates. Changing the temperature of the build plate can change its state so that it can stick while printing and release when done. Heated build plates sometimes have other advantages as well.

Temperature settings are related to the material being used to print with, so no recommendation can be made here.

Retraction

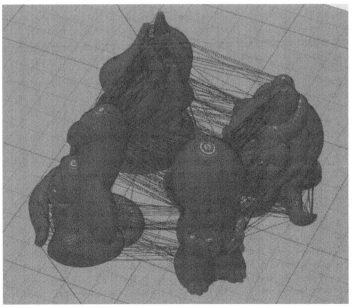

If the model prints and it separates into two or more islands on a particular layer, or if you're printing more than one part at a time, then as the nozzle travels between the two parts it needs to pull the plastic out of the nozzle while traveling to avoid drooling material in-between. This is called **retraction**. Retraction settings include how far and how fast to pull the plastic out. This setting can reduce the amount of stringiness, or little hairs, that are being deposited on a print.

It may seem like a high retraction is always a good idea, but retracting too far can cause melted plastic to get jammed in the feed tube.

The retraction settings vary depending on the type of 3D printer and material being printed with.

Fan Speed

If your 3D printer has a blower fan to cool off the plastic as it leaves the nozzle you may have control of settings for the **fan speed** in your slicer. Some materials, like PLA, prefer a constant blast of moving air for best results. Others, like ABS, do better with light fan or none at all. If a print has tall and thin parts, including support scaffolds, a high fan speed may cause it to shake, so turn it down in those cases.

Optimal fan speed settings also vary per material.

Skirt/Brim

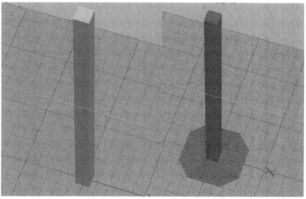

Skirt and brim are both the same idea and in some slicers are combined into one setting. The **skirt** is an outline drawn around the part, usually to prime the nozzle for printing. Some printers have default GCode including preparation of the nozzle in other ways, so a skirt may not be necessary.

However, if that skirt is widened to include many outlines, and the distance from the part is dropped to zero so it touches the part, the skirt becomes a **brim**. Brims are attached to the printed part and will need to be removed after the print is done. Usually they break right off.

A brim can be very useful. Something with a very small footprint on the build plate may not adhere well during printing. But give it a brim and now it's got a solid surface to stick to the build plate with. Or, if your print is experiencing curling due to material shrinkage which is causing it to lift off the build plate, a brim can improve adhesion or take the brunt of the lifting so the main part stays stuck down while printing.

When and how to use brims are an advanced technique for 3D printer users that can take print success to a new level.

Custom GCode

```
G1 X91.354 Y173.797 E58.7392
G1 X113.308 Y151.842 E59.1298
G1 X98.947 Y165.496 E59.3790
G1 X91.533 Y172.911 E59.5109
G92 E0
G1 E-1.5000 F1800
; layer 41, Z = 6.135
; inner perimeter
G1 X90.213 Y173.214 F4800
G1 Z6.135 F1002
G1 E0.0000 F1800
G92 E0
G1 X175.683 Y91.952 E1.4836 F2700
G1 X189.787 Y106.786 E1.7410
G1 X104.317 Y188.047 E3.2246
G1 X90.213 Y173.214 E3.4821
; outer perimeter
G1 X89.507 Y173.196 F4800
G92 E0
```

The output of a slicer is GCode, which is a special set of instructions that describes every motion and action the 3D printer can perform. GCode is actually just plain text, though it can be a bit difficult to decipher because it's not written for humans. Often, you will have to look up the codes and what they do online.

Slicers allow you to take a section of GCode and insert it into the print wherever you want it. In this way, special behavior can be added to a print. Examples include: stopping the print mid-way to change filament or inserting an object into the print, then continuing, or drawing a specific pattern at the start of the print to prime the nozzle. Custom GCode can also move the extruder head to a specific place after printing to automatically remove the print from the platform.

While inserting GCode has great potential, it's also very advanced and often, strictly speaking, not necessary.

Get to Know Your Slicer

That wraps up the most common settings that most slicers share and will give you a strong basis for using slicers to prepare models for 3D printing. If you're ever confused about a slicer setting, remember you have this handy reference for the most common settings.

Slicers are the first part of the 3D printing process. Hopefully they're not seen as inconvenient. Instead, look at them as the power to take full advantage of your 3D printer to make things real.

10

How to Use Slicers by Example

Video links:

Combined:
https://www.youtube.com/watch?v=H7brUq9DOdY

Cura: https://www.youtube.com/watch?v=QnLuJNDCofA

Cura 2: https://www.youtube.com/watch?v=5GgiolAdoJs

Slic3r: https://www.youtube.com/watch?v=IuTbpOkK610

Simplify3D:
https://www.youtube.com/watch?v=uFDZHFMZ0pk

Slicing is the first step in the 3D printing process. For most FFF 3D printers, the slicer is a piece of software running on a computer outside the 3D printer. Your computer. In this chapter, we'll go through the process of downloading, installing, and using the slicer to make a GCode file that the 3D printer can use to create a 3D print.

Even if you don't have a 3D printer, there's nothing stopping you from loading a slicer on your computer and experimenting with slicing a 3D model. If you do have a 3D printer, then this step is required.

Downloading the Example Model

To make this interesting we're going to use a file that requires some advanced settings to get right. To start follow this link and download the file that is there:

http://www.thingiverse.com/thing:33344

This is the tornado vase by Alessandro Ranellucci, modified from Martijn Elserman's original design. This model will work with all slicers and will create a vase... if printed with some clever use of advanced settings.

Downloading Your Slicer

What slicer you'll be using may vary. If your 3D printer's manufacturer suggests a slicer or has their own you should probably use that one. If not you've got a choice. The most popular slicers right now are: Cura, Slic3r, and Simplify3D. To complicate matters even more, Cura made a major change when it switched to version 2, but a lot of 3D printers still recommend the older version.

Cura - https://ultimaker.com/en/products/cura-software/list (look for 15.04.06, the last version before 2)

Cura 2 - https://ultimaker.com/en/products/cura-software

Slic3r - http://slic3r.org/

Simplify3D - https://www.simplify3d.com/

Each slicer has its strengths, and different people have their preferences. But for this project they all have settings that will allow the proper slicing of this model. In this chapter, we'll assume you're using one of these slicers on a Windows-based machine. If that's not the case these instructions can still be used generally, but you'll have to adjust for your particular circumstances.

Once you've downloaded your choice of slicer, run the installer and bring the slicer up on your computer.

If during this chapter one of the slicers has a significant difference from the steps listed it'll get its own section to give separate instructions. Like this:

Slic3r Notes

Slic3r does not have an installer. Instead you'll have to choose a folder on your computer and unzip the slic3r-mswin-xXX-X-X-X.zip file there. Your desktop is an okay choice for this, but it is recommended to unzip to a folder on the C:/ drive and put a shortcut to the slic3r.exe on your desktop.

Setting Up for Your Printer

Slicers are designed to work with many different 3D printers and their various sizes, configurations, and nuances. Because each type of 3D printer is a little different, the first thing a slicer has to do is configure itself for your 3D printer. Fortunately, it's easy to do this.

Run your slicer for the first time.

Cura and Cura2 Notes

The first time you run Cura you will be given a wizard with menus to help you set up your printer. Cura comes preloaded with profiles for many printers. Simply choose your printer from the list and Cura does the rest. If your printer isn't on the list you can choose "other" and input the configuration manually. Check with your 3D printer's manufacturer to find out the specific setting you'll need to use.

If you are doing this without a 3D printer, then pick the printer at the top of the list.

Slic3r Notes

Slic3r does not come with any pre-configured printers. Instead, you input the individual settings that pertain to your printer. Check with your 3D printer's manufacturer to find out the specific settings you'll need to use.

If you are doing this just for practice, Slic3r isn't the best slicer to start with.

Simplify3D Notes

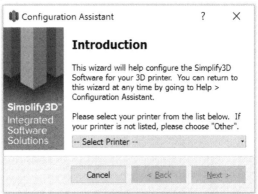

The first time Simplify3D starts up you will see the configuration assistant. (You can get to this any time in Simplify3D from the Help menu.) Simplify3D comes preloaded with profiles for many printers. Choose your printer from the drop-down menu and Simplify3D does the rest. If your printer isn't on the list you can choose "other" and input the configuration manually. Check with your 3D printer's manufacturer to find out the specific setting you'll need to use.

It is unlikely you will be using Simplify3D if you don't already own a 3D printer, but if you do you can pick any 3D printer.

Getting Acquainted with Your Slicer

As mentioned before, each slicer is slightly different, while they also have many things in common. However, since they're all different, here's the breakdown:

Cura Notes

Cura has the following components on its main screen:

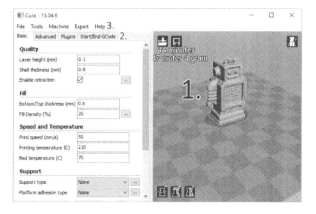

1. Virtual Build Space - This gives you a visual representation of where your 3D models will be positioned in your build space. At the top-left of this window are buttons for loading in STLs and saving GCode. At the top-right is the view options. At the

bottom are tools for manipulating the selected model including rotating, scaling, and mirroring the model.

    a. Right-click and drag, rotates the view

    b. Shift+Right-click and drag, pans the view

    c. Moving the scroll-wheel zooms the view in and out

2. Settings Tabs - Here are the settings for your printer, organized in tabs. All the settings mentioned in the previous chapter can be found here.

3. Menu Bar - Other options are available in the menus at the top of Cura.

Cura2 Notes

Cura2 has the following components on its main screen:

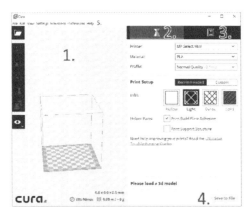

1. Virtual Build Space - This gives you a visual representation of where your 3D models will be located and positioned in your build space. On the left are icons for, from top-to-bottom, loading 3D models, manipulating 3D models, and changing the view.

    a. Right-click and drag rotates the view
    b. Shift+Right-click and drag pans the view
    c. Moving the scroll-wheel zooms the view in and out
2. Print Settings Tab - These are the settings that can be manipulated to alter the print.
3. Printer Tab - If a printer is connected to your computer via USB, this tab will allow you to access it directly.
4. Save to File Button - This button saves the GCode output.
5. Menu Bar - Other options are available in the menus at the top of Cura2.

Slic3r Notes

Slic3r has the following components on its main screen:

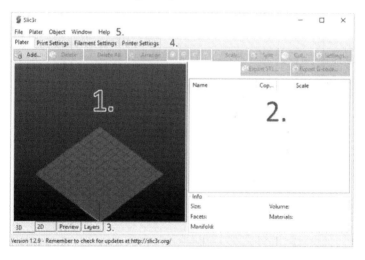

1. Virtual Build Space - This gives you a visual representation of where your 3D models will be located and positioned in your build space.
    a. Left-click and drag to rotate the view

      b.   Right-click and drag to pan the view

      c.   Moving the scroll-wheel zooms the view in and out

2. Models List - The list of all 3D models loaded and some information about them. Above this list are buttons to manipulate the 3D models including scale, breaking models into their component parts, and splitting big models up for printing.

3. Views Tabs - You can switch between the different views of the virtual build space.

4. Settings Tabs - You can switch between the view of the plate and the settings of the print, filament, and printer.

5. Menu Bar - Other options are available in the menus at the top of Slic3r.

Simplify3D Notes

Simplify3D has the following components on its main screen:

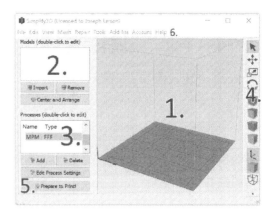

1. Virtual Build Space - This gives you a visual representation of where your 3D models will be located and positioned in your build space.

a. Left-click and drag rotates the view
b. Right-click and drag pans the view
c. Moving the scroll-wheel zooms the view in and out

2. Models List - Here is the list of the 3D models you have loaded into Simplify3D for printing. Below the list are buttons for Importing and Removing objects from the build space, as well as a button to automatically arrange the parts on the print bed so they're not overlapping, called "Center and Arrange".

3. Process List - Simplify3D keeps all the settings you use in in processes. Simplify3D can do a lot with multiple processes, but this example will keep it simple.

4. Object and View Manipulation Tools - These tools allow for quick manipulation of the objects on the build plate and adjusting the 3D view of the Virtual Build space. These tools include selecting, moving, scaling, rotating objects, as well as, further down the tool shelf, direct machine control and customizing supports. Hover over an icon to find out what it does.

5. Prepare to Print Button - This is the button you will press when you're ready to turn the 3D models into GCode.

6. Menu Bar - All of Simplify3D functions and many more can also be accessed from the menu bar including some limited mesh manipulation tools.

Loading and Manipulating an STL file

Once the slicer is installed and running, the next step is to give it something to slice. You can either import the STL model file from the menu or you can find the 3D file in your file system and drag-and-drop it to your slicer window.

Import the *golvend_fixed.stl* 3D model downloaded before, into your slicer. It should be in your downloads folder.

With the STL loaded in you will see a preview of it in your virtual build space.

If the tornado model is too big for your printer, some STL manipulation may be necessary. Using the object scale tool the tornado model can be resized.

Cura Notes
Scale in Cura goes from 0 to 1, so, for example, 45% of the original size will be 0.45.

Cura2 Notes
Cura2 will automatically scale models that are too big to fit in your build area, and will tell you that it's done so. You can still click on the model and select on the scale icon to type in the scale if you wish to.

Slic3r Notes
While it seems like Slic3r has fewer options for manipulating loaded models, like rotating and moving models on the build plate, the options do exist. For instance, in the *Object* menu in the top menu bar or by right-clicking on the model you get options for rotating and flipping the models. And under *File->Preferences* you can turn off the option to auto-center objects on your build plate.

Simplify3D Notes
The scale, rotation, and positioning tools in the sidebar in Simplify3D allow for manipulating the model with the

mouse. If you prefer exact numeric control you can double-click on the model to pull up the model details and type in location, scale, and rotation information.

Creating the GCode and Previewing the Print

Without changing any of the print settings it's time to make a slice of the model and preview how it will print. It is always a good idea to carefully look over the preview before sending it to the printer.

Cura Notes

Click on the View Mode button in the upper left-hand corner, choose "Layers", and wait for the view to load. Along the right side a slider appears. Scrubbing this slider up and down allows for previewing the print layer-by-layer. Some features, like solid layers and infill, won't be visible until you're looking at the specific layer.

Cura2 Notes

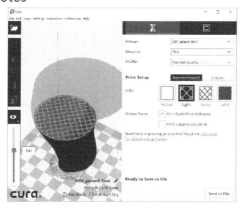

Click on the View Mode button in the lower left-hand side, choose "Layers" and wait for the view to load. Along the left side a slider appears. Scrubbing this slider up and down allows for previewing the print layer-by-layer. Some features, like solid layers and infill, won't be visible until you're looking at the specific layer.

Slic3r Notes

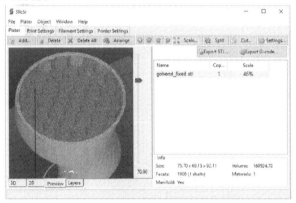

Click the Preview tab under the Virtual Build Space to see a preview of your model. Along the right side is a slider. Scrubbing this slider up and down allows for previewing the print layer-by-layer.

Simplify3D Notes

Click on the *Prepare to Print* button in the lower left-hand corner and the model will be sliced. The program will change to the GCode preview. In this mode Simplify3D has all-new information and buttons.

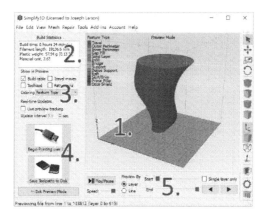

1. 3D GCode preview - Your model appears as it will when it prints, with the layers, shells, and infill that will be a part of the final print.

2. Build Statistics - Information including an estimated time to build the print and how much material will be used.

3. Preview Settings - You can change how the preview is displayed and what information is available in the GCode preview.

4. Printing Buttons - These buttons will allow you to start a print either over USB or saving the GCode to a file that can be transferred to your printer.

5. Layer Scrubbers - These sliders allow a preview of the print mid-process so you can preview that the infill, shells, and everything are just as you want them.

The same toolbar on the side and top menu is also present, but only the options related to adjusting the view are active in this mode.

Adjusting the Settings

Now that we've successfully sliced the model, if we printed it like this, it wouldn't be as intended. This is meant to be a vase, hollow in the middle with an open top. But it's not meant to be that way by changing the model. You're supposed to manipulate the slicer to make it into a vase.

Change the slicer so it prints this model with:

- Infill = 0%
- Top Layers = 0
- Bottom Layers = 10 or 2mm
- Shells = 4 or 2mm

Cura Notes

- To the left of the 3D view, click the Basic settings tab
- Set Shell thickness (mm) to 2
- Set Bottom/Top Thickness to 2
- Set Fill Density % to 0
- Click on the ... button next to the Fill Density % setting

- In the Expert Config menu that pops up uncheck the Solid Infill Top box

Note that for Cura the Shell Thickness and Bottom/Top thickness is a measurement of millimeters. Cura automatically calculates, based on your nozzle diameter and layer thickness, how many of each of these to add. Also note that the layer view is updated as you work.

Cura2 Notes
- On the right-hand side under Print Setup click the button that says Custom
- Expand the Shell accordion menu
- Change the Wall Thickness to 2
- Change the Top/Bottom Thickness to 2
- Expand the Infill accordion menu
- Change the Infill Density to 0%

That takes care of most of the settings, but the top of the print is still filled in. Cura hides this setting deeper.

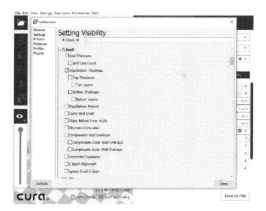

- Hover over the Shell accordion menu to make the gear icon appear
- Click the gear icon

- In the Settings Visibility menu that comes up check the Top Thickness and Bottom Thickness check boxes
- Click Close
- Set the Top Thickness setting to 0

One of Cura2's biggest strengths is that while you can control every minutiae of the printing process, it hides most of those settings giving first-time users a much friendlier experience. And it doesn't make them difficult to find for experienced or growing users who don't mind learning.

Slic3r Notes

- Click the Print Settings tab
- Under General change the Layer Height to something between 0.2 and 0.1
- Change Perimeters to 4
- Change Solid Layers Top to 0
- Change Solid Layers Bottom to 10
- Under Infill change Fill Density to 0
- Click the Printer tab to go back to Preview mode to verify the changes took place

Slic3r has an expert mode that provides some more settings and lays things out in categories with a sidebar to help you navigate them. For the improved navigation alone many people prefer expert mode. But all the settings this project needs are available in simple mode.

Simplify3D Notes

- If you're still in the GCode preview, click the Exit GCode Preview button.
- Click the Edit Process Settings button.
- Move the Infill Percentage slider all the way to the left (0%)
- Click the Show Advanced button.
- Click the Layer tab.
- Set the Top Solid Layers to 0
- Set the Bottom Solid Layers to 6
- Set the Outline/Perimeter Shells to 4
- Click Ok

Printing the Vase

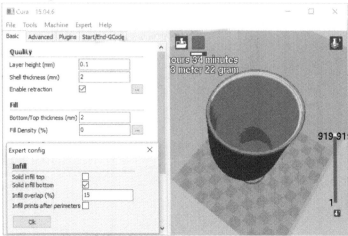

Now that the settings are correct, create the GCode and Preview the print again. Notice now that the model is hollow with an open top, a perfect vase. This model does not require any supports because of clever control of gradual overhangs. If your printer is connected to your computer via USB you can start printing. Or you can save the GCode file and get that file to your printer, either on an SD card or some other way to start printing.

Cura Notes
The slicing is done on-the-fly, so all you have to do is click the Save Toolpath in the upper-left of the 3D view to save the GCode file.

Cura2 Notes
The slicing is done on-the-fly, so all you have to do is click the Save to File button in the lower-right to save the GCode file.

Slic3r Notes

The slicing is done on-the-fly, so all you have to do is click the *Export G-code* button above the models list to the right to save the GCode file.

Simplify3D Notes

Click the *Begin Printing over USB* or *Save Toolpaths to Disk* button on the GCode preview, depending on how your printer is set up.

Printing over USB versus SD card printing

When it's an option, why choose to print over the USB vs saving the GCode to an external media like an SD card and inserting that card into the printer? Each method has its advantages, and in the end it usually boils down to a personal preference. Ultimately the choice is yours.

Printing Over USB

Printing over USB is great because it means you can start your print at the push of a button. However, it has some disadvantages. Your printer must be located within a USB cable's length of your computer at all time and especially during a print. Because your computer is feeding each instruction to the printer as it needs them, if your computer or the USB connection fails during the print your print will fail. Also, USB printing is sometimes slower with pauses in the process while the computer reads the state of the printer.

Printing From an SD Card

Printing from an SD card involves the extra step of removing the media from your printer, inserting it into your computer, copying the file, and transporting it back to the printer. Some printers allow you to do this over Wi-Fi, which can be preferable, but it's still an extra step. However, it frees your printer from your computer so you can put the printer and its noise in any well-ventilated area you want. Because your printer isn't waiting to be fed commands from your computer it can sometimes print faster, more reliably, and smoother.

The Final Print

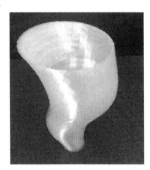

Remember, you've manipulated your settings to make this print happen. You'll have to reset them if you don't want all future prints to be vases.

Cura2 Notes

This is one area where Cura2 really shines. Every setting you change from the default has a reset icon next to it, so you never have to look for the recommended setting and it's easy to reset back to base.

Conclusion

Controlling your slicer means controlling your 3D printer. It allows you to tune how long a print will take, how much material you want to use, and other aspects of your print. Sometimes startling results can be achieved by manipulating the settings, like in the case of vase printing. Also, many slicers have advanced features that make them desirable over other slicers. Becoming acquainted with those settings will allow you to become a 3D printing master.

11

Where to Find 3D Files to Print

"Share and Enjoy' is the company motto of the hugely successful Sirius Cybernetics Corporation Complaints Division, which now covers the major land masses of three medium-sized planets and is the only part of the Corporation to have shown a consistent profit in recent years.

Now that you know how to make prints with your 3D printer, where do you find 3D files to print? Designers have been making 3D print files for years and many of them are shared online, most of them for free.Sites like Thingiverse, Youmagine, Pinshape, MyMiniFactory, 3DUpNDown, 3DSha.re, and many others host tens of thousands of 3D files that you can download and print.

One Search Engine
Becoming aware of the many sites out there can simplify matters, but searching each one individually can be

troublesome. A well-worded web search might turn up the results you want, but it might also turn up results on websites that don't allow 3D file downloads, or don't host models that are for 3D printing.

Fortunately, there are a few search engines that focus on 3D printable designs and limit their results to sites those designs. The top 3 search engines for 3D models are:

- Yeggi.com
- STLFinder.com
- Yobi3d.com

Searcher Beware

These search engines can save you a lot of time, but there are still pitfalls to look out for.

Not every 3D model that claims it can be 3D printed has been tested yet. If you find a 3D file to download, but only computer renders exist and no one has printed it yet, you may be the first. And the first often discovers problems that the designer didn't foresee.

On the other hand, if a 3D model has been printed many times it's safe to assume you're going to have a good time.

Not every 3D model posted is the most recent version of that model. Especially on Thingiverse, check for "remixes", where people who have taken a design and iterated it to make a better version. A few seconds to identify if you're using a latest and best version can save you frustration. If the website doesn't identify remixes for you, and you see multiple versions that you can't determine which is the latest, check the timestamp. More recent is, often times, better.

Lastly, not everything has been modeled yet, and not every model is available for download. Even if you see a 3D print of something, there's no guarantee that you can find the 3D model online. Not every 3D designer wants their model printed by anyone. Sometimes their reason is commercial. Sometimes there are concerns for another person's safety. Sometimes they just don't want to deal with the headache of uploading, describing, and taking pictures of their print to upload them. Whatever the reason, if a designer doesn't make their models available, there's little you can do.

In the case where exactly what you want doesn't exist, it may be time for the next step: learning 3D design.

But that's a topic for another book.

Acknowledgements

First of all, thank you to my wife. No paragraph at the end of a book can adequately pay you back for all you've done and enabled me to do.

The 3D printing community online is more than a group of like-minded individuals. You're all like a family to me. Sometimes a little too much like family.

A very special thank you goes out to Douglas Adams for being such a formative part of my adolescent years. You may have passed, but you'll never be gone. Quotes from Douglas Adams' Hitchhiker's Guide trilogy of books (far more than just 3 books, by the way), with varying degrees of relevancy, pepper this work.

About the Author

My name is Joe and I'm known on YouTube as the 3D Printing Professor. I'm an award-winning 3D designer, author, blogger, and YouTuber. I've been using all kinds of 3D printers for years, both professionally and in my personal life. I have thousands of hours of 3D printing and have experienced every success and problem along the way.

If you want to know more please check me out on YouTube, Blogger, and Social media. I love when people reach out and ask questions. It always inspires me to do more.

https://www.youtube.com/user/mrjoesays

https://joes3dworkbench.blogspot.com/

https://twitter.com/3DPProfessor

https://www.facebook.com/3DProfessor/

Until we meet again, so long and thanks for all the prints!

27984480R00053

Printed in Great Britain
by Amazon